THE SILLY KIDS JOKE BOOK

Cooper the Pooper

TABLE OF CONTENTS

INTRODUCTION

Well, hello there, fellow jokester!

Did you know that you have some of my best jokes right in the palm of your hand?

Well, you do — and they are guaranteed to get some laughs.

It was only a couple of years ago that I was spending all of my time laying in the sun, digging through trash, and chasing cats. But then I realized that there are lots of kids just like you who spend all of their time glued to the screen of their phones rather than playing with *me*.

How boring!

So, while thinking of some ways you can have amazing fun with your friends and family, I started writing books. Honestly, what better way to have some fun than by sharing a couple — or a couple of hundred — jokes?

Many of these jokes have become favorites at home. My owner and his kids love sharing them after a long day at school. They even get some laughs out of Grandma, and she doesn't laugh at *anything*. They are seriously that good.

So, whether you are looking for some jokes to share with your best friend or want to get your grandma to crack a big smile, there is something in here for everyone.

I hope you are as excited as I am to dive into some of the funniest jokes on the planet — but make sure you don't laugh too hard, or you might break a funny bone!

ANIMAL JOKES

01

Where do cows go for entertainment?
- **The moo-vies**

02

Where do you find a dog with no legs?
- **Right where you left him!**

03

What do you get when you cross a Labrador and a magician?
- **A Labracadabrador!**

04

Why are penguins socially awkward?
- **Because they can't break the ice.**

05

Why do you never see elephants hiding in trees?
- **Because they are really good at it.**

06

Why do fish live in salt water?
- **Because pepper makes them sneeze!**

07

What kind of facial hair does a moose have?

· **A moostash**

08

Why can't you trust zookeepers?

· **They love cheetahs.**

09

How do you know if there's an elephant under your bed?

· **Your head hits the ceiling.**

10

What do you call a cold bird in winter?

· **A brrr-d!**

11

Why don't koalas count as bears?

· **They don't have the right koalafications.**

12

On what day of the week do chickens hide?

· **Fri-day**

13

Why do seagulls fly over the sea?

- **If they flew over the bay, they would be bagels.**

14

What do you call a bear with no teeth?

- **A gummy bear**

15

How do elves learn how to spell?

- **They study the elf-abet.**

16

What do you call a dinosaur that is sleeping?

- **A dino-snore**

17

What do you call a fly without wings?

- **A walk!**

18

Why aren't dogs good dancers?

- **They have two left feet.**

19

What's worse than finding a worm in your apple?

- **Finding half a worm**

20

Why can't you trust the king of the jungle?

- **Because he's always lion.**

21

How do you get a squirrel to like you?

- **Act like a nut.**

22

Why does a giraffe have a long neck?
- **Because his feet stink.**

23

Why did the chicken cross the playground?
- **To get to the other side.**

24

What do you call a dead fly?
- **A flew**

25

Why don't crabs share their food?

• **Because they're shellfish.**

26

What's the biggest moth in the world?

• **A mam-moth!**

27

How do Indian and African elephants talk to each other?

• **On an elephone!**

28

What are the strongest sea creatures?

• **Mussels**

29

How do you make an egg roll?

• **Push it!**

30

Why is it impossible for a leopard to hide?

• **Because he will always be spotted.**

31

What do you call a bee that's having a bad hair day?

- **A frisbee**

32

What is the strongest creature in the world?

- **The snail; it carries its whole house on its back.**

33

What do you do when you find a blue elephant?

- **Cheer it up.**

34

What is the best way to catch a fish?

- **Have someone throw it to you.**

35

What do you call a horse that lives in the house next to you?

- **A neeeeeeigh-bor.**

36

Why did the puppy sit in the sun?

- **He wanted to be a hot dog!**

37

What did the bee say when he got home from work?

- **Honey, I'm home!**

38

Why are baby cows so cute?

- **They are adora-bull!.**

39

Why did the dog cross the road?

- **To get to the barking lot..**

40

What do polar bears eat for lunch?

- **Ice berg-ers!**

41

What did the worm say to the other worm when he came home late?

- **Where in earth have you been?**

42

Why can't dinosaurs clap?

- **Because they're extinct.**

43

What do you call a monkey at the North Pole?

• **Lost**

44

What do you call five giraffes?
• **A high five**

45

What do you call an elephant that doesn't matter?
• **An irrelephant**

46

Which animal writes the best?
• **A pen-guin**

47

What do sea monsters eat?
• **Fish and ships.**

48

What do you call a blind dinosaur?
• **A do-you-think-he-saw-us.**

49 Why don't dinosaurs eat clowns?

- **Because they taste funny.**

50 What do you call a sheep with no legs?
- **A cloud**

51 What is a cow's favorite place?
- **A moo-seum.**

52 Why are elephants big and gray?
- **If they were small and purple, they would just be grapes..**

53 What do you call a monkey that flies?
- **A hot-air baboon**

54 What do you call an elephant that's in a phone booth?
- **Stuck.**

55

What did the duck say to the waiter?

· **Put it on my bill.**

56

What kind of bug is in the FBI?

· **A SPY-der**

57

Why do dragons sleep during the day?

· **So they can fight knights!**

58

What would a bear say if they got confused?

· **I barely understand.**

59

Why should you not let a bear operate the remote?

· **He will keep pressing the paws button.**

60

What's gray and goes around and around?

· **An elephant in a washing machine.**

61

What do you call an ant that won't go away?

· **Perman-ant**

62

Why did the giraffe get bad grades?

· **He always had his head in the clouds.**

63

What happens when you annoy a rabbit?

· **You get a bad hare day.**

64

What type of bee can't make up its mind?

· **A maybe**

65

How does a farmer count his cows?

· **With a cow-culator**

66

Where does a turtle go when it's raining?

· **A shell-ter!.**

67

What do you call a cow that plays the guitar?

- **A moo-sician!**

68

What do you call a lizard that performs hip-hop?

- **A rap-tile.**

69

What do you call a turkey after Thanksgiving?

- **Lucky!**

70

What do you call a bee that comes from America?

- **A USB**

71

What's the hardest thing about learning to ride a horse?

- **The ground**

72

Why are giraffes such good fathers?

- **Because they're someone you can look up to.**

73

What do you call a bird on an airplane?

- **Lazy**

74

Why do they put bells on cows?

- **Because their horns don't work.**

FOOD
JOKES

fried egg

75

What's the best thing to put into a pie?
- **Your teeth**

76

What do you call a sad strawberry?
- **A blueberry**

77

What do you give a sick lemon?
- **Lemon-aid**

78

Why was the apple so lonely?
- **Because the banana split.**

79

What did the egg say to another egg?
- **Have an eggselent day!**

80

Why was the baby strawberry crying?
- **Because her parents were in a jam.**

81

What did the banana say to the dog?

• **Nothing; bananas can't talk.**

82

Why didn't the orange win the race?

• **It ran out of juice!**

83

Where do you learn to make ice cream?

• **Sundae school**

84

Why did the melon jump into the lake?

• **Because he wanted to be a watermelon.**

85

How does the moon say that she doesn't want to eat?

• **She's full.**

86

Where do hamburgers go to dance?

• **They go to the meat-ball.**

87

How many cherries grow on a cherry tree?

- **All of them**

88

What kind of candy is never on time?

- **Choco-LATE**

89

What kind of lunch do moms never prepare in the morning?

- **Their own**

90

Why shouldn't you tell an egg a joke?

- **Because it might crack up.**

91

What did the father tomato say to the baby tomato while they were out for a walk?

- **Ketchup!**

92

Yesterday a man threw a glass of milk at me. What did I do?

- **I thought, "How dairy!"**

93 What did the potato say, before getting skinned?

- **"This does not a-PEEL to me."**

94 What's the best way to help starving monsters?

- **Give them a hand.**

95 Why do the French like to eat snails?

- **Because they don't like fast food.**

96 What do you call two bananas?

- **A pair of slippers**

97 What tower eats a lot?

- **The I Full Tower!**

98 Why shouldn't you fall in love with a pastry chef?

- **They'll just DESSERT you.**

99 Why did the baker quit making donuts?

- **He was just sick of the hole thing!**

100 What do snowmen eat for breakfast?

- **Snowflakes**

101 When do you go on red and stop on green?

- **When you are eating a watermelon.**

102 What do you get if you cross a cheetah with a burger?

- **Fast food**

103 Why are teddy bears never hungry?

- **Because they are always stuffed.**

104 What do you take before every meal?

- **A seat**

105

What did the time traveler do when he was still hungry after dinner?

- **He went back four seconds.**

106

When do astronauts eat?

- **At launch time!**

107

What do you get when you cross a monkey with a peach?

- **An ape-ricot**

108

What did the calculator say to the math student?

· **You can count on me.**

109

Why did the student eat his homework?

· **Because the teacher told him it was a piece of cake.**

110

Why did the kid bring a ladder to school?

· **Because he wanted to go to high school.**

111

Why did the math book look so sad?

· **Because it had so many problems.**

112

Why does the sun have to go to school?

· **To get brighter**

113

How did you find school today?

· **It was there when I got off the bus.**

114

What did the pen say to the other pen?
- You're ink-redible.

115

Why didn't the teddy wear shoes to school?
- He liked to have bear feet.

116

- What is the funniest time of the school day?
- Laughter-noon

117

What do you need to bring to music class?
- A note-book

118

Why did the chemistry teacher stop telling jokes?
- She never got a reaction.

119

What do you get when you cross a teacher with a tiger?
- I don't know, but you'd better behave in its class.

120

What is a snake's favorite subject?
- **HISStory**

121

What do you get when you cross a teacher and a vampire?
- **Lots of blood tests**

122

Why was six afraid of seven?
- **Because seven ate nine.**

123

Where were pencils invented?
- **PENCIL–vania**

124

What did you learn in school today?
- **"Not enough; I have to go back tomorrow."**

125

What class does a butterfly like best?
- **Mothematics**

126

Why did the music teacher get locked in his piano?

· **The keys were stuck on the outside.**

127

What is a witch's favorite subject in school?

· **Spelling.**

128

How do you get straight A's?

· **By using a ruler!.**

129

Why did the kid study in the airplane?

· **Because he wanted a higher education.**

130

Why didn't the sun go to college?

· **Because it already had a million degrees.**

131

Why did the teacher put on sunglasses?

· **Because her students were so bright.**

132

Why was school easier for cave people?

- **Because there was no history to study**

133

I can't go to school today. I don't feel well. Where don't you feel well?

- **In school**

134

Why is History the fruitiest school subject?

- **Because it is full of dates!**

135

My dad: You missed school yesterday!

- **Me: To tell you the truth, I didn't really miss it.**

136

The teacher shouted at me for something I didn't do.

- **My homework.**

137

Why did the lamp go to school?

- **He wasn't very bright.**

138

How did the beauty school student do on her manicure test?

- **She nailed it.**

139

Why did the broom get a poor grade in school?

- **Because it was always sweeping during class.**

140

Why couldn't the student finish the geometry problem?

- **She didn't look at it from a different angle.**

141

Why was the principal so worried?

- **There were too many rulers at school.**

142

Teacher: "Don't you know you can't sleep in my class?"

- **Student: "I know. But maybe if you were just a little quieter, I could."**

143

What is a chalkboard's favorite drink?

- **A hot chalk-olate!**

144

What do you call a person who keeps on talking when people are no longer interested?

- **A teacher**

145

Why do magicians do so well in school?

- **They're good at trick questions.**

146

Why did the music teacher need a ladder?

- **To reach the high notes**

147

Why isn't there a clock in the library?

- **Because it tocks too much.**

148

What's the best place to grow flowers in school?

- **In kinder-garden**

149

Why did the teacher draw on the window?

- **Because he wanted his lesson to be very clear.**

150

Why did the Cyclops close his school?

- **Because he only had one pupil.**

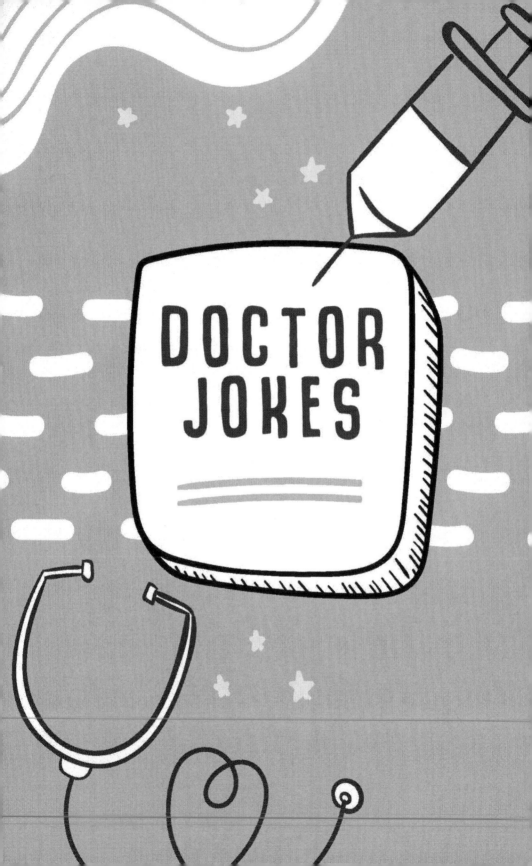

151 Why did the computer go to the doctor?
- **It had a virus..**

152 What did Walt Disney say when we went to the doctor?
- **Dis-knee hurts!**

153 Where does a ship go when it's not feeling well?
- **To see the dock-tor**

154 What time do you go to the dentist?
- **At tooth-hurty**

155 Why did the leaf go to the doctor?
- **It was feeling green.**

156 Why are you staring at your hamburger?
- **My doctor told me to watch what I eat.**

157

"Doctor, I've broken my arm in two places."

· "Well, don't go back to those places anymore."

158

Why did the doctor install a knocker on his door?

· He wanted to win the No bell prize.

159

Where do people go when they have two broken legs?

· Nowhere!

160

Why did the cookie go to the nurse?

· Because he felt crumby.

161

What do you call a dentist who fixes crocodile's teeth?

· Totally crazy

162

Why did the boy tiptoe past the medicine cabinet?

· He didn't want to wake the sleeping pills!

163

Why did the vet cross the road?

- **It wanted to learn more about the lives of chickens!**

164

Did you hear about the phone that went to the dentist?

- **It had a Bluetooth.**

165

What did the man say to the X-ray technician after swallowing some money?

- **Do you see any change in me?**

166

Doctor: I have some bad news and some very bad news. The lab called with your test results. They said you have 24 hours to live.

Patient: 24 hours! That's terrible! What's the very bad news?

Doctor: I've been trying to reach you since yesterday.

167

Patient: Doctor, I get heartburn every time I eat birthday cake.

Doctor: Next time, take off the candles.

168

Why did the mattress go to the doctor?

· **It had spring fever**

169

What don't you want to hear in the middle of surgery?

· **"Where's my watch?"**

170

What did the doctor prescribe to the man who couldn't stop breaking wind?

· **A kite**

171

A skeleton went to the doctor. The doctor looked at the skeleton and said,

· **"Aren't you a little late?"**

172

What did the balloon say to the doctor?
· **I feel light-headed.**

173

Why do surgeons wear masks?

· **So no one will recognize them when they make a mistake.**

174

What did the banana go to the doctor?
- **It wasn't peeling well.**

175

Doctor: I've got very bad news — you've got cancer and Alzheimer's.
Patient: Well, at least I don't have cancer.

176

What do you call a student that got C's all the way through med school?
- **Hopefully not your doctor.**

177

Woman: My husband swallowed an Aspirin by mistake. What should I do?
Doctor: Give him a headache!

178

How did you know that doctor was fake?
- **She had good handwriting.**

179

Why did the king go to the dentist?
- **To get his teeth crowned!**

180

Why did the library book go to the doctor?

· **It needed to be checked out**

181

"Doctor, doctor, will I be able to play the violin after the operation?"
"Yes, of course.."
"Great! I never could before!"

182

Why should you never lie to an X-ray technician?

· **He can see right through you!**

183

Why did the doctor take a red pen to work?

· **In case he wanted to draw blood**

184

What's it called when a hospital runs out of maternity nurses?
· **A mid-wife crises**

185

Why did the tailor go to the doctor?
· **He had pins and needles.**

186

Doctor, doctor! I'm scared of Father Christmas!

· **You're suffering from Claus-trophobia!**

187

Man: "Doctor, my wife is pregnant, and her contractions are only two minutes apart!"
Doctor: "Is this her first child?"
Man: "No, this is her husband!"

188

Patient: "I'm starting to forget things!"
Doctor: "Since when have you had this condition?"
Patient: "What condition?"

189

When I went to see the doctor, he remarked that he hadn't seen me in a while.

· **So, I said that I have been ill.**

190

Patient: "Doctor, doctor, I've only got 50 seconds to live."
Doctor: "Just give me a minute."

191

Why did the author go the doctor?

· **His editor told him he needed the appendix removed.**

192

Patient: "Doctor, my back hurts when I wake up in the morning. What should I do?"
Doctor: "Wake up in the afternoon then."

193

How did the computer catch a cold?
· **It left its Windows open!**

194

What did the doctor say to the volcano?
· **You need to quit smoking!**

195

What did the doctor say was wrong with the car mechanic?
· **He'd had a breakdown!**

196

When does a doctor get mad?
· **When he runs out of patients!**

197

Why are ghosts such bad liars?
- Because you can see right through them..

198

What do ghosts like to eat in the summer?
- I scream.

199

What do you call a ghost's mom and dad?
- Transparents

200

Why are ghosts so happy in elevators?
- Because it lifts their spirits.

201

Why did the ghost make the cheerleading squad?
- They needed team spirit.

202

How do ghosts greet each other?
- "How do you boo?"

203

Where do ghosts buy their food?

· **At the ghostery store**

204

What did the ghost teacher say to the class?

· **"Look at the board, and I will go through it again."**

205

What was the ghost's best position?

· **Ghoulkeeper**

206

What's the one room a ghost doesn't need in its house?

· **A living room**

207

What are ghosts' favorite trees?

· **Ceme-trees**

208

Who did the scary ghost invite to his party?

· **Any old friend he could dig up!.**

209

What do you call a ghost who haunts fireplaces?
- **A toasty ghosty!**

210

On what day are ghosts most scary?
- **Fright-day!**

211

What do you do when 50 ghosts visit your house?
- **You hope it's Halloween!**

212

Why didn't the skeleton go to the party?
- **He had no body to go with!**

213

What do ghosts say to their children?
- **Spook when you're spooken to!**

214

What did the daddy ghost say to the baby ghost?
- **Fasten your sheet belt!**

215

What's a zombie's favorite bean?

- **A human bean**

216

What do ghosts do at sleepovers?

- **They tell scary human stories!**

217

What's a witch's favorite make-up?

- **Ma-scare-a!**

218

What do you call a witch with chickenpox?

- **An itchy witchy**

219

What kind of streets do zombies prefer?

- **Dead ends!**

220

Do zombies eat popcorn with their fingers?

- **No, they eat their fingers separately!**

221

Did you hear about the monster who ate too many houses?

- **Yes, he was homesick!.**

222

What does Dracula like to watch on TV?

- **Neck-flix!**

223

What position does Dracula like to play in baseball?

- **Bat!.**

224

How do skeletons tell their future?

- **They look at their HORRORscope!.**

225

What's a vampire favorite type of boat?

- **A blood vessel!**

226

Why did the vampire need mouthwash?

- **Because he had bat breath..**

227

What's it called when a vampire has trouble with his house?

- **A grave problem.**

228

Which fruit is a vampire's favorite?

- **A neck-tarine**

229

What do Italian ghosts have for dinner?

- **Spook-hetti!.**

230

Why did the skeleton climb up the tree?

- **Because a dog was after his bones!**

231

How did the skeleton know it was going to rain on Halloween?

- **He could feel it in his bones.**

232

Why are skeletons so calm?

- **Because nothing gets under their skin.**

233

Where do ghosts live?

- **They don't.**

234

What did the ghost say to the other ghost?

- **Do you believe in humans?**

235

Why didn't the scarecrow eat dinner?

- **He was already stuffed!**

236

What do baby ghosts wear on Halloween?

- **Pillowcases**

237

What kind of key does a ghost use to unlock his room?

- **A spoo-key!**

238

What do young ghosts write their homework in?

- **Exorcise books**

239

Why did the ghost go to the hair salon?

- **To make herself boo-tiful!**

240

Did you hear the joke about the roof?
- **Never mind; it's over your head.**

241

What did the traffic light say to the car?
- **Don't look. I'm about to change.**

242

Why should you never trust stairs?
- **Because they're always up to something**

243

How do billboards talk?
- **In sign language**

244

Why shouldn't you tell jokes about dead cellphones?
- **They just don't work.**

245

What did one elevator yell to the other?
- I'm falling!

246

Why didn't the lamp sink?
- **It was too light.**

247

What bow can't be tied?
- **A rainbow!**

248

Why was the airplane ill?
- **He had the flew!**

249

Why do bicycles fall over?
- **Because they're two-tired.**

250

What is an elevator's favorite exercise?
- **Push-ups**

251

What kind of guitar always has a cold?

- **An achoo-stic**

252

What do you call a can opener that doesn't work?

- **A can't opener**

253

Why did the toilet paper roll down the hill?

- **To get to the bottom**

254

Why was the car so smelly?

- **It had too much gas.**

255

Do the buses here run on time?

- **No, they run on wheels.**

256 What did the candle say to the envelope?

- **Seal you later.**

257 What kind of building weighs the least?

- **A lighthouse**

258 Why was the broom late?

- **It over-swept.**

259 How did the mobile phone propose to his girlfriend?

- **He gave her a ring.**

260 Why did the cannon have trouble finding work?

- **Because it kept getting fired.**

261 What did one hat say to the other?

- **"You stay here, and I'll go on ahead."**

262

What did one knife say to the other knife?
- **"You're looking sharp today!"**

263

Why was the remote control annoyed?
- **Because everyone was pushing its buttons**

264

Why did the phone wear glasses?
- **Because it lost its contacts.**

265

Why didn't the telephone pass the eighth grade?
- **It wasn't a smart phone.**

266

What's a recycling bin's favorite reading?
- **Litter-ature**

267

What toy is always in the bathroom?
- **The TOY-let!**

268

Why did the credit card go to jail?
- **It was guilty as charged.**

269

What makes the calendar look so popular?
- **It has so many dates.**

270

Why did the picture go to jail?
- **It was framed!**

271

What did the stamp say to the envelope?
- **"Stick with me, and we'll go places together."**

272

What did the blanket say to the bed?

- **"Don't worry; I've got you covered."**

273

Why did the laptop get glasses?

- **To improve its web sight.**

274

What do you call a boat that has a hole on the bottom?

- **A sink**

275

Where do library books like to sleep?

- **Under their covers!**

276

Why did they bury the battery?

- **Because it was dead.**

277

Why do candles always go on the top of cakes?

- **Because it's hard to light them from the bottom.**

278

What did the limestone say to the geologist?

- **"Don't take me for granite!"**

279

What happened to the man who crossed a witch with a clock?

- **He got a brooms-tick!**

280

What gives you the power to walk through a wall?

- **A door**

281

Why couldn't the flower ride its bike to school?

- **Its petals were broken.**

282

Where do TVs go for vacation?
- **Remote islands**

283

Why did the airplane get sent to his room?
- **It had a bad altitude.**

284

Why are robots never afraid?
- **Because they have nerves of steel.**

2 8 5

Why can't your hand be 12 inches long?
- **Because then it would be a foot.**

2 8 6

Which hand is better to write with?
- **Neither! It's better to write with a pencil.**

2 8 7

How do they answer the phone at the paint store?
- **Yellow!**

2 8 8

What do you call a funny mountain?
- **Hill-arious!**

2 8 9

What time is it when a ball goes through the window?
- **Time to get a new window**

290

What did the left eye say to the right eye?

· **Between us, something smells!**

291

What goes up, but doesn't come back down?

· **Your age**

292

If it takes two men to dig a hole in one day, how long would it take for one man to dig a half of a hole?

· **There is no such thing as a half of a hole.**

293

Why did the man run around his bed?

· **He was trying to catch up on sleep.**

294

Why do you go to bed every night?

· **Because the bed won't come to me.**

295

Why was the burglar so sensitive?

- **He takes things personally.**

296

Why did the girl throw a stick of butter out the window?

- **She wanted to see a butterfly.**

297

Why did Johnny jump up and down before he drank his juice?

- **The carton said to "shake well before drinking."**

298

Why is there a fence around the cemetery?

- **People are dying to get in.**

299

Did you hear about the guy whose whole left side was cut off?

- **He's all right now.**

300

What do you call the wife of a hippie?

- **A Mississippi**

301

Why did the boy take the ruler to bed?

- **He wanted to see how long he slept.**

302

Why shouldn't you believe a person in bed?

- **Because they are lying.**

303

What can be served but never eaten?

- **A tennis ball**

304

Which word in the dictionary is spelled incorrectly?

- **Incorrectly**

305

Where do liars learn to lie?

- **At the lie-brary**

306

Why doesn't anyone want to be friends with a clock?

- **All it does is tock-tock-tock.**

307

Why does underwear last longer than any other clothing?

- **Because it's never worn out.**

308

Which is faster: cold or heat?

- **Heat is; you can catch a cold.**

309

What happened to the two comedians who got married?

- **They lived happily ever "laughter!"**

310

What do you call it when a really skinny person visits Hawaii?

- **A TOO WEAK vacation**

311
If you had $1, and you asked your father for another, how many dollars would you have?
- One

312
Don't spell "part" backwards. It's a trap.

313
I didn't like my beard at first, but then it grew on me.

314
What kind of button won't unbutton?
- A belly button

315
How do you cut a wave in half?
- You use a sea-saw.

316

What does every birthday end with?
- **The letter Y**

317

What do you call a guy lying on your doorstep?
- **Matt**

318

How do you learn to be a trash collector?
- **Just pick it up as you go along.**

319

Did you hear the joke about the high wall?
- **Yes, and I still can't get over it.**

320

What did you get for your birthday?
- **Older**

321

Did you hear the joke about the germ?
- **Actually, never mind. I don't want to spread it around.**

322
Why didn't the invisible man accept the job offer?
• **He just couldn't see himself working there.**

323
Did you hear about the actor who fell through the floor?
• **It was just a stage he was going through.**

324
What birthday should you celebrate by going camping?
• **Your TENT-h birthday!**

325
Why did the man put sugar under his pillow?
• **So he would have sweet dreams.**

326

Knock, knock!
Who's there?
Water.
Water who?
Water you doing in my house?!

327

Knock, knock!
Who's there?
Annie.
Annie who?
Annie body home?!

328

Knock, knock!
Who's there?
Lettuce.
Lettuce who?
Lettuce in; it's cold out here!

329

Knock, knock!
Who's there?
Nana.
Nana who?
Nana your business!

330

Knock, Knock!
Who's there?
Justin.
Justin who?
Justin time for lunch!

331

Knock, Knock!
Who's there?
Hike.
Hike who?
I didn't know you liked Japanese poetry!

332

Knock, Knock!
Who's there?
To.
To who?
No, it's "to whom!"

333

Knock, Knock!
Who's there?
Candice.
Candice who?
Candice joke get any worse?!

334

Knock, knock!
Who's there?
Alex.
Alex who?
Alex-plain when you open the door!

335

Knock, knock!
Who's there?
Ya.
Ya who?
No thanks; I use Gmail.

336

Knock, knock!
Who's there?
I am.
I am who?
Don't you even know who you are?

337

Knock, knock!
Who's there?
Spell.
Spell who?
W-H-O!

338

Knock, knock!
Who's there?
Canoe.
Canoe who?
Canoe come and play?
I'm bored!

339

Knock, knock!
Who's there?
Kenya.
Kenya who?
Kenya feel the love tonight?

340

Knock, knock!
Who's there?
Razor.
Razor who?
Razor hand, and dance the
boogie!

341

Knock, knock!
Who's there?
Amos.
Amos who?
A mosquito!

342

Knock, knock!
Who's there?
Icing.
Icing who?
Icing so loudly so everyone can hear me!

343

Knock, knock!
Who's there?
Hatch.
Hatch who?
Bless you!

344

Knock, knock!
Who's there?
Tank.
Tank who?
You're welcome!

345

Knock, knock!
Who's there?
Voodoo.
Voodoo who?
Voodoo you think you are, asking me so many questions?

346

Knock, knock!
Who's there?
Opportunity.
Opportunity who?
Opportunity doesn't knock twice!

347

Knock, knock!
Who's there?
Doctor.
Doctor who?
Hey, that's my favorite TV show!

348

Knock, knock!
Who's there?
Ketchup.
Ketchup who?
Ketchup with me, and I'll tell you!

349

Knock, knock!
Who's there?
A herd.
A herd who?
A herd you were home, so I came over!

350

Knock, Knock!

Who's there?

Somebody too short to ring the doorbell!

351

Knock, Knock!

Who's there?

Yourself.

Yourself who?

Your cell phone's ringing, so you better answer it!

352

Knock, Knock!

Who's there?

Donut.

Donut who?

Donut ask me — I just got here!

353

Knock, Knock!

Who's there?

Ireland.

Ireland who?

Ireland you my umbrella; you'll need it.

354

Knock, Knock!
Who's there?
Juno.
Juno who?
Juno that I'm out here, right?

355

Knock, Knock!
Who's there?
Ice cream.
Ice cream who?
Ice cream if you don't let me inside!

356

Knock, Knock!
Who's there?
Barbie.
Barbie who?
Barbie Q Chicken!

357

Knock, Knock!
Who's there?
Nobel.
Nobel who?
No bell; that's why I knocked!

358

Knock, Knock!
Who's there?
Burglar.
Burglar who?
Burglars don't knock!

359

Knock, Knock!
Who's there?
Dozen.
Dozen who?
Dozen anyone want to let me in?

360

Knock, Knock!
Who's there?
Sing.
Sing who?
Whooo-ooo-ooo!

361

Knock, Knock!
Who's there?
Doris.
Doris who?
Doris locked; that's why I'm knocking!

362

Knock, Knock!
Who's there?
Double.
Double who?
W!

363

Knock, Knock!
Will you remember me in a year?
Yes.
Will you remember me in a month?
Yes.
Will you remember me in a week?
Yes.
Will you remember me in a day?
Yes.
Knock, knock!
Who's there?
See, you forgot me already!

364

Knock, Knock!
Who's there?
Bean.
Bean who?
Bean a while since I saw you!

365

Knock, Knock!
Who's there?
Police.
Police who?
Police, may I come in?

366

Knock, knock!
Who's there?
Mikey.
Mikey who?
Mikey doesn't fit in the key hole

367

Knock, knock!
Who's there?
Wire.
Wire who?
Wire you asking me this?

368

Knock, knock!
Who's there?
Amish.
Amish who?
Awe, I miss you too.

369

Knock, knock!
Who's there?
Goat.
Goat who?
Goat to the door and find out.

370

Knock, Knock!

Who's there?

Kanga.

Kanga who?

No, Kangaroo!

371

Knock, Knock!

Who's there?

Anita.

Anita who?

Anita borrow a pencil!

372

Knock, Knock!

Who's there?

Watson.

Watson who?

Watson TV tonight?

373

Knock, Knock!

Who's there?

Sweden.

Sweden who?

Sweden the coffee;
it's too bitter!

374

Knock, knock!
Who's there?
Figs.
Figs who?
Figs the doorbell; it's broken!

375

Knock, knock!
Who's there?
Wanda.
Wanda who?
Wanda ring if you'll open the door!

376

Knock, knock!
Who's there?
Arya.
Arya who?
Arya ready to go swimming?

377

Knock, knock!
Who's there?
Witches.
Witches who?
Witches the way home?

378

Knock, Knock!
Who's there?
Max.
Max who?
Max no difference — just open the door!

379

Knock, Knock!
Who's there?
Dewey.
Dewey who?
Dewey have to listen to all this knocking?

380

Knock, Knock!
Who's there?
I love.
I love who?
I don't know; why don't you tell me?!

381

Knock, Knock!
Who's there?
Europe.
Europe who?
No, you're a poo!

382

Knock, Knock!

Who's there?

Scold.

Scold who?

Scold outside; let me in!

383

Knock, Knock!

Who's there?

Cotton.

Cotton who?

Cotton a trap!

384

Knock, Knock!

Who's there?

Ali.

Ali who?

Alligator!

385

Knock, Knock!

Who's there?

Ruff.

Ruff who?

Ruff, ruff, it's your dog!

386

Knock, Knock!
Who's there?
Jacken.
Jacken who?
Jacken Jill went up the hill.

387

Knock, Knock!
Who's there?
Alien.
Alien who?
How many aliens do you know?

388

Knock, Knock!
Who's there?
Hada.
Hada who?
Hada great time!

389

Knock, Knock!
Who's there?
Sir.
Sir who?
Sir-prise! I have more jokes for you.

390

Knock, Knock!
Who's there?
Noah.
Noah who?
Noah good place we can get something to eat?

391

Knock, Knock!
Who's there?
Jo.
Jo who?
Jo King!

392

Knock, Knock!
Who's there?
Sofa.
Sofa who?
Sofa, these have been good knock-knock jokes!

393

Knock, Knock!
Who's there?
Luke.
Luke who?
Luke through the peephole and find out!

394

Knock, knock!

Who's there?

Vanna.

Vanna who?

Vanna go see a movie tonight?

395

Knock, knock!

Who's there?

Solomon.

Solomon who?

It's just me — I'm SOLO, MAN!

396

Knock, knock!

Who's there?

Stan..

Stan who?

Stan back! I'm knocking this door down!

397

Knock, knock!

Who's there?

Heaven.

Heaven who?

Heaven seen you in a while.

398

Knock, knock!
Who's there?
Gorilla.
Gorilla who?
Gorilla me a burger, please.
I'm hungry.

399

Knock, knock!
Who's there?
Parrot.
Parrot who?
Parrot who? Parrot who?
Parrot who?

400

Knock, knock!
Who's there?
Dawn.
Dawn who?
Dawn do anything that I
wouldn't do!

401

Knock, knock!
Who's there?
Needle.
Needle who?
Needle little help right now!

96

402

Knock, knock!
Who's there?
Cereal.
Cereal who?
Cereal pleasure to meet you!

403

Knock, knock!
Who's there?
Lena.
Lena who?
Lena little closer, and I'll tell you another joke.

404

Knock, knock!
Who's there?
Champ.
Champ who?
Champ-oo the dog. He needs a bath!

405

Knock, knock!
Who's there?
Akita.
Akita who?
I need Akita open the door.

406

Knock, Knock!
Who's there?
Says.
Says who?
Says me. You looking for trouble?

407

Knock, Knock!
Who's there?
Ozzie.
Ozzie who?
Ozzie you later, alligator!

408

Knock, Knock!
Who's there?
Thermos.
Thermos who?
Thermos be some way to get you to open the door!

409

Knock, Knock!
Who's there?
Philip.
Philip who?
Philip up my cup; I'm thirsty!

410

Knock, Knock!
Who's there?
Ooze.
Ooze who?
Ooze in charge around here?

411

Knock, knock!
Who's there?
Howard
Howard who?
Howard I know?

412

Knock, Knock!
Who's there?
Answer the door, and you'll find out!

413

Knock, Knock!
Who's there?
Yukon.
Yukon who?
Yukon say that again!

414

Knock, Knock!
Who's there?
Harold.
Harold who?
Harold are you, young lady?

415

Knock, Knock!
Who's there?
Al.
Al who?
Al come back later!

416

Knock, Knock!
Who's there?
Sam.
Sam who?
Sam person whose been knocking for 10 minutes now.

417

Knock, Knock!
Who's there?
Stan.
Stan who?
Standin' here in the rain, can you let me in?

418

What kind of tree fits in your hand?

- **A palm tree**

419

What did one volcano say to the other?
- **I lava you!**

420

What did the big flower say to the little flower?
- **Hi, bud!**

421

What day of the week are most twins born?
- **Twos-day!**

422

What did the dad chimney say to the little chimney?
- **You're too young to smoke!**

423

What did the one tube of glue say to the other?
- **"Let's stick together."**

424

What was wrong with the wooden car?
- **It wooden go!**

425

Have you ever tried to eat a clock?
- **No, it's very time consuming.**

426

How do we know that the ocean is friendly?
- **It waves!**

427

What does a raincloud wear under her dress?
- **Thunderwear!**

428

What are the strongest days of the week?
- **Saturday and Sunday. The rest are weak days.**

429

Where does Superman love to shop?
- **At the supermarket!**

430

Why can't you ever tell a joke around glass?
- **It could crack up.**

431

What's the difference between a guitar and a fish?
- **You can tune a guitar, but you can't tuna fish.**

432

Why did Johnny throw the clock out of the window?
- **Because he wanted to see time fly.**

433

What do you call an old snowman?
- **Water**

434

Why is it so windy inside a stadium?
- **There are hundreds of fans.**

435

What's scarier than a monster?
- **A momster**

436

How did the barber win the race?
- **He knew a short cut.**

437

What did the beach say to the tide when it came in?
- **Long time, no sea.**

438

Why can't you give Elsa a balloon?
- **She'll let it go.**

439

Why can't Cinderella play soccer?
- **Because she's always running away from the ball.**

440

Why did the clock go to the principal's office?

• **For tocking too much.**

441

Why do scissors always win a race?
• **Because they take a shortcut!**

442

Why couldn't the sailor learn his alphabet?
• **Because he always got lost at C.**

443

Why did the king go to the bathroom?
• **He wanted to sit on the throne.**

444

What did one toilet say to the other?
• **You look a bit flushed!**

445

What do you call it when the butcher gives you the wrong order?
- **A mis-STEAK**

446

What did the one-dollar bill say to the ten-dollar bill?
- **"You don't make any cents."**

447

Did you hear about the two guys who stole a calendar?
- **They each got six months.**

448

Why did the burglar take a shower?
- **He wanted to make a clean getaway.**

449

What did the girl ocean say to the boy ocean when he asked her out on a date?
- **Shore!**

450

Why is a bad joke like a broken pencil?
- **Because it has no point.**

451

What do you call a smart group of trees?

- **A brain-forest**

452

What washes up on very small beaches?
- **Microwaves!**

453

What do you call a boy named Lee, who no one talks to?
- **Lonely**

454

How do you throw a party on Mars?
- **You planet.**

455

Why is Peter Pan always flying?
- **Because he never lands.**

456

What is the best day to go to the beach?
- **Sunday, of course!**

457

What did the nose say to the finger?
- **Quit picking on me!**

458

Why does Humpty Dumpty love autumn?
- **Because he always has a great fall.**

459

Want to hear a roof joke?
- **This first one's on the house.**

460

How does a scientist freshen her breath?
- **With experi-mints!**

461

Why did Darth Vader turn off one light?
- **He prefers it on the dark side.**

462

How did Benjamin Franklin feel when he discovered electricity?
- **Shocked!**

463

What did the tree say to the wind?
- **Leaf me alone!**

464

What do you call a fairy that doesn't like to shower?
- **Stinkerbell**

465

What do skeletons say before a meal?
- **"Bone appetite."**

466

Why are circles so smart?
- **Because they have 360 degrees.**

467

On which side of the house do pine trees grow?
- **On the outside**

468

What is the color of the wind?
- **Blew**

469

Why is England the wettest country?
- **Because the queen has reigned there for years.**

470

Why are mummies so bad at paying attention?
- **They're too wrapped up in themselves.**

471

Why couldn't Dracula sleep?
- **Because of his coffin.**

472

Why are Olympians bad DJs?
- **They're always breaking records.**

473

What happens to ice when it gets mad?

- **It has a meltdown.**

474

I was going to get a brain transplant. What happened?
- **They changed my mind.**

475

What falls in winter, but never gets hurt?
- **Snow!**

476

Why couldn't the pirate play cards?
- **Because he was sitting on the deck.**

477

Why aren't planets social?
- **They need their space.**

478

Where do zombies go swimming?
- **The Dead Sea**

479

What did one ice cube say to the other?
- **"I'm cooler than you!"**

480

Why did the burglar enter the singing contest?
- **He wanted to steal the show.**

481

How do you scare a snowman?
- **Show him a hair dryer.**

482

What do you call a frightening wizard?
- **Scary Potter!**

483

Why was the nose sad?
- **Because it didn't get picked.**

484

What is the best part of a boxer's joke?

- **The punch line**

485

What is the richest kind of air?
- **A millionaire**

486

Who keeps the ocean clean?
- **The mermaid**

487

Why did the skeleton drink eight glasses of milk every day?
- **Milk is good for the bones.**

488

Why didn't the girl trust the ocean?
- **There was something fishy about it.**

489

What letters are not in the alphabet?
• **The ones in the mail**

490

What country makes you shiver?
• **Chile**

491

What do snowmen do in their spare time?
• **They just chill.**

492

What do you call a snowman's kids?
• **Chilled-ren**

493

What has keys but no doors, space but no rooms, and you can enter but never leave?
• **A keyboard!**

494

On what day do monsters eat people?
- **Chewsday!**

495

What did one flame say to the other?

- **"We're a perfect match."**

496

How does a very small person say goodbye?
- **With a microwave**

497

What Disney character thinks the most?
- **Thinkerbell**

498

What time of year do people get injured the most?
- **In the fall.**

499

Why did the woman become an archaeologist?
- **Because her career was in ruins.**

500

What did the tree say after a long winter?
- **What a re-leaf!**

501

What did one leaf say to another?
I'm falling for you!

502

I was wondering why the ball was getting bigger.
- **Then it hit me.**

503

My friend recently got crushed by a pile of books. Who could he blame?
- **He's only got his shelf to blame.**

504

What's the best part about living in Switzerland?
- **Not sure, but the flag is a big plus.**

505

I just left my job. I couldn't stay after what my boss said to me.
What did she say?
- **You're fired.**

FINAL WORDS

First and foremost, thanks for taking
the time to read my book!

I hope you got as many laughs from reading
it as I did from writing it (which I must admit,
was quite a lot).

The best thing about a big book of jokes like this
is that it won't expire. This means that you can
share them over and over again with all your
friends and family, leaving a trail of loud laughs
and big smiles behind you.

So, what are you waiting for? Go ahead and
make your friends and family giggle — because
honestly, nothing would make me happier.

Made in the USA
Las Vegas, NV
22 October 2021